AF429492

SALAZAR RISING

Salazar Rising:
The Establishment of Portugal's New State
Jamie Stewart Jones

© Jamie Stewart Jones 2024

ISBN 9798227413130

CPHRC Editorial Services
506-508 Strathmartine Road
Dundee DD39BR
Scotland
cphrc@cphrc.co.uk

SALAZAR RISING

The Establishment of Portugal's New State

Jamie Stewart Jones

CPHRC editorial services

Thank you

Thank you for purchasing this book. We hope that you find the content valuable and engaging.

As you dive into the pages, we would be grateful if you could take a moment to leave an honest review on Amazon. Your feedback is essential to us and helps others make informed decisions about their reading choices.

Honest reviews, whether positive or constructive, play a crucial role in supporting our small business and enabling us to improve.

Thank you once again for your purchase and for being part of our journey. We look forward to hearing your thoughts and hope you enjoy the book!

To leave a review, please follow these steps:
1. Go to Amazon and search for the product name or ASIN.
2. Navigate to the product page.
3. Scroll down to the reviews section.
4. Click on "Write a customer review" to leave your feedback.

A brief note

This essay was written about 25 years ago, was presented at a seminar and then found its way into a box that was gradually forgotten over the years.

I recently decided to have a clear out of old boxes that were cluttering up a space I suddenly decided I needed. That is when I rediscovered a large collection of papers that I had written back when I was researching and writing about the Portuguese First Republic. This is one of these papers, which I think deserves to see the light of day again.

Jamie Stewart Jones
Dundee, October 2024

António de Oliveira Salazar

Salazar Rising: The Establishment of Portugal's New State

Any investigation into legitimation processes leading to the establishment of the Portuguese New State must take cognisance of the fact Salazar's regime both emerged from and succeeded the military dictatorship that had overthrown the parliamentary republic in May 1926 and suspended the 1911 constitution.

According to Costa Pinto (1992: 88), recognising this fact helps prevent the investigator from confusing 'the political and ideological origins of the authoritarian regime and its leaders, with those of the political and ideological agents who overthrew liberalism in 1926'.

However, it is important to note that Salazar was, as Finance Minister between 1928 and 1932, one of the most important members of the military dictatorship's cabinet, and that the dictatorship itself was not replaced until after the approval of Salazar's proposed constitution through a national plebiscite in March 1933.[1]

Salazar only assumed the portfolio of President of the Council of Ministers (Prime Minister) in the previous July, taking over from the military administration of General Domingos de Oliveira (Payne: 1973: 666).

The reason Costa Pinto feels it pertinent to issue a word of warning regarding this matter is, ultimately, bound up in the general and persistent controversy, not to mention confusion, over the ideological and socioeconomic nature of the authoritarian regimes that appeared in many European states during the interwar period (Payne 1980: 3-21).

One of the major problems for students of the six-year interregnum period prior to the establishment of the New State (Estado Novo) was the difficulty in making sense of the heterogeneous coalition that united under the umbrella of the 28 May Movement.

---

[1] For a discussion of the plebiscite held on 19 March 1933, see Kay (1970), Derrick (1937) or Fryer and McGowan (1961). As Kay notes (49n1), disagreement over the degree of support for the new constitution exists. However, given the prevailing situation and the circumstances under which the plebiscite was conducted, the result was largely a foregone conclusion.

Salazar's diagnosis:
A new vision, 1928-30

Although led by senior military officers, the 28 May Movement was supported by individuals and organisations representing almost the entire spectrum of Portuguese political opinion—from representatives of the weak and fragmented left, through opposition republicans (those who were outside the hegemonic Democratic faction) to monarchists, conservatives, Integralists and fascists (Payne 1973: 572).

While many of the coup's military supporters undoubtedly admired the earlier example set by Primo de Rivera, their Spanish comrades in arms, and believed they were fulfilling their historic mission as true guardians of the nation's will in embarking on such an undertaking, there is very little evidence that they had any plans or ideas for the future organisation of Portuguese society.

The coup's leaders defined their behaviour and justified their actions in purely pragmatic and immediate terms.

For example, they claimed they were intervening to prevent a civil war between the republicans and the monarchists and to restore governmental authority: beyond this, there was nothing, so effectively they were 'a regime in search of a formula' (Wiarda 1979: 94).

It was this lack of ideas and the fundamental failure of the military leaders to develop a coherent ideology or strategy that left them susceptible to the influence of the competing factions that coolest under the 28 May Movement's wide shadow (Costa Pinto 1986).

Much of the available literature illustrates the contradictory nature of the dictatorship's support, demonstrating how it could never represent more than a transitory step on the path to something that was somehow less ephemeral and more stable (Payne 1973; Wiarda 1979; Costa Pinto 1986; Derrick 1938: 44-51; Egerton 1943: 100-1).

In effect, it implicitly suggests that due to its failure to elaborate a coherent and consistent policy, the dictatorship was unable to sustain a situation in which it would be possible for it to present itself as a legitimate alternative to the system that it had successfully overthrown.

As it transpired, Portuguese society did not have to wait too long before divisions within the new regime exposed themselves, and the competing factions slugged it out with each other over the spoils of victory.

According to Costa Pinto, 'The 28 May Movement was itself marked at the beginning by a rapid succession of coups that immediately led to the alienation of the liberal republican wing and soon after to the leader himself' (1986).

While much of the blame for the dictatorship's instability can be placed at the door of the authoritarian right and its efforts to influence policy,[2] it should also be noted that before 1928, the dictatorship failed to control the nation's budgetary deficits.

Cotta's economic investigation into Salazar's New State shows that in the financial year immediately following the coup, Portugal's annual deficit had swollen to 641,616 contos.[3]

This was an increase of 425% over the First Republic's final year's deficit.

Moreover, while it is true that the annual deficit was reduced to 181,377 contos in the succeeding financial year, this figure was still almost 60% higher than the parliamentary republic's average annual deficit between 1910 and 1926 (Cotta 1937: 2).[4]

[2] Costa Pinto (1986), following Payne's 'tripartite typology of rightist political groups' (see Payne 1980: 14-21), believes the radical right should shoulder much of the blame For the disorder prevalent during the interregnum period of 1926 to 1928. He states that by attempting to dominate the regime through the formation, in 1927, of the National 28 May League, they did much to undermine its essentially conservative nature by pushing it in a more radical direction. Forcing the dictatorship in a more right-wing direction only served to highlight the still deeply heterogeneous nature of its support, thereby alienating many important pillars of support (such as the moderate republicans).

[3] One conto is equal to 1000 escudos. Assuming an exchange rate of 133.95 escudos to £1 sterling, this amounts to a sterling equivalent of approximately £4,789,966.

[4] The average annual deficit for the 16 years of the parliamentary republic, calculated using Cotta's figures, was 116,355 contos.

The dictatorship's failure to deal adequately with any of Portugal's many problems and its essentially *ad hoc* nature ultimately created the circumstances through which Salazar was able to manoeuvre himself and his supporters into positions of dominance within the military regime.

Salazar believed that he, and he alone, had the ability to pull the nation out of the mess that was the legacy of 18 years of misgovernment.

When, in 1928, President Carmona called on Salazar to rescue the military regime, he accepted.

However, it was to be an acceptance hedged with important qualifications:

> ...Please do not offer me your thanks. To me, it means such a great sacrifice... It is a sacrifice that I am willing to make for my country in serene and calm discharge of a conscientious duty... I know quite well what I want and where I am going, but let it not be insisted that I shall reach the goal in a few months. For the rest, let the country study, let it suggest, let it object and let it discuss, but when the time comes for me to give orders, I shall expect it to obey (Salazar 1939: 43-5).

In addition, as a condition of his acceptance of the portfolio, he made four demands that effectively placed the government under the tutelage of his department and made him the real power in Portugal.[5]

The fact that this dictatorship felt obliged to accede to Salazar's demands says much about the predicament in which its leaders perceived themselves.

Salazar's vision and tenacity successfully infused the dictatorship with a sense of direction and a strategy for the future.[6]

Through a combination of creative accounting and deflationary policies, he managed to balance the budget by the end of 1928, his first year in control.

By 1937, Marcelo Caetano, one-time Integralist and author of Salazar's 1933 constitution, was able to claim that since 1928, the balanced budget, 'which for a century had been an impossibility... had become an

---

[5] The four conditions were: 1. That each government department shall undertake to limit and organise its services within the total amount allotted by the Ministry of Finance; 2. Any measure adopted by the various government departments that may directly affect the state's receipts and expenditure shall be discussed beforehand, and an agreement arrived at with the Ministry of Finance; 3. The Ministry of Finance shall be entitled to place its veto on all increases of current or ordinary expenditure and expenditure for development purposes, for which the necessary credit operations shall only be undertaken with the knowledge of the Ministry of Finance; 4. The Ministry of Finance undertakes to collaborate with the other departments in measures that may be adopted to reduce expenditure or collect revenue, which will be organised as far as possible on uniform principles. Salazar (1939: 44).

[6] For a hagiography of Salazar's influence on the dictatorship, the reader is directed towards Derrick (1938), Egerton (1943) and Kay (1970). For a more critical appraisal, see Costa Pinto (1992).

inflexible rule of our financial life and a solid basis of the whole political structure...' (Cotta 1937: ix).

Salazar used his influence astutely and almost immediately began to outline his vision for the future.

In October 1929, he was to make an important speech to the country's municipal leaders in which he outlined his own plan, one that was intended to initiate 'into Portuguese political life the use of the official language of *truth*, in place of the former language of official *truths*' (Salazar 1939: 48).[7]

In this speech, Salazar is emphatic in asserting that rights cannot exist without corresponding duties.

He said the government has a duty towards the nation to be honest, open and free from intrigue or falsehood, while the nation's corresponding duty towards the government is to be truthful and 'not to exaggerate or to misrepresent'.

Salazar goes on to state that if the nation fails in its duty of honesty, then the government will fail and that failure will be the sole responsibility of the nation for its lack of cooperation.

In an attack, not merely on political parties but also on the tendency for cliques to emerge and attempt to control government for their own ends, he goes on to define the nation in organic,

---

[7] This quote is from the translator's introduction to the speech: 'A policy of truth. A policy of sacrifice. A national policy'.

as opposed to legalistic terms: it is a 'historical and social reality, embracing individuals, families, private and public bodies'.

Thus, the concept of *nation* is imbued with a highly ethical value comprising cultural and historical traditions and charged with the political task of enhancing this harmony and defending it from parties, cliques and class divisions: 'Our motto then shall be 'All for the nation: nothing against the nation'' (Salazar 1939: 59).

Salazar is clearly elaborating a vision of Portugal's future that seeks to place as much distance between his ideals and those that were, in his view, prevalent during the First Republic.

In doing so, he makes his first clear attack on the legitimacy of the parliamentary republic:

> When we see how certain doctrines, seemingly sincere but harmful in reality, are being disseminated all over the world, we feel that the rebirth of our national consciousness, supported by a truly national policy, is absolutely necessary in order to prevent the destruction of interests vital to our prosperity (1939: 61).

The guiding principle of the First Republic's leaders was the sanctity of the individual, a notion Salazar denounced as 'morally and materially destructive'.

Morally destructive because it diminished social life to such an extent that it became little more than a series of economic relationships in which 'the worker had been degraded to the level of a machine' (Cotta 1937: 11), and materially destructive because it encouraged mortgaging the future for the comforts of the present (Salazar 1939: 55).

In May 1930, at a meeting celebrating the fourth anniversary of the dictatorship, Salazar was to deliver another speech in which he dealt with both the example set by the politicians of the parliamentary republic and, significantly, the dictatorship's record.

Although still only Minister of Finance, Salazar was by this time the real power in Portugal, and his words were keenly followed and eagerly reported by a largely supportive press, and while he may have enjoyed some popular support for his policies,[8] it is nonetheless apparent that he felt it necessary to move beyond merely attacking the record of the First Republic.

In this speech, Salazar begins to attempt to distance himself from the dictatorship in the nation's mind.

While denouncing the parliamentary republic,

[8] Due to the lack of popular participation, a historic trait of Portuguese politics, it is difficult to quantify the degree to which Salazar enjoyed popular support. However, what qualitative material there is (for example, newspapers) suggests that, at least in the narrow newspaper-buying circle, his policies did command a certain degree of favour.

he also had to somehow delegitimise the military dictatorship in such a manner as would not compromise his attempt to imbue his own project with legitimacy.

Salazar was to drive home his belief the dictatorship could be nothing more than a merely temporary step on the road towards Portugal's reconstruction.

He chastises those who unthinkingly criticised the regime for its failure and asks them to cast their minds back to the situation that demanded the military to act 'in order that we may render justice to the present'.

He described the First Republic as an era of disorders, liberally sprinkling his speech with such nouns as 'confusion', 'disruption', 'failure', 'disharmony' and 'indifference'.

It was a time when there was no political prestige, of financial ineptitude, economic decline and social insecurity.

He takes pains to remind his audience that the parliamentary republic was a government that was incapable of establishing order, unable to secure peace, and one that presided over a society that was steadily descending into anarchy:

> For when the weakness of governments
> cannot efficiently guarantee the rights
> of each person, the people take upon

> themselves individually to defend their lives, their interests and their property as best they can, or else they are vanquished, downtrodden and held in terror by audacious minorities who violate justice without fear of reprisal (Salazar 1939: 73).

When reading this speech, one must be aware of the audience it is directed towards.

Those who attended the meeting at which it was delivered were army and navy officers largely sympathetic towards, if not active participants in the dictatorship.

The wider audience was the newspaper-buying public, which, in a nation where more than half the population were illiterate, was primarily restricted to a small, educated and property-owning elite.

These very people would have most to lose whether to be a return of the liberal system.

The dictatorship saved Portugal from these disorders and retrieved the nation's honour by restoring the rule of law.

However, the restoration of order required the temporary suspension of rights without any concomitant suspension of duties and obligations.

The suspension of these rights was intended to be a measure that would ensure the restoration of the idea that the relationship between the government and those who are government is fundamentally symmetrical: 'by suspending rights that the nation did not possess... The dictatorship provided the government with the necessary conditions to undertake a vast and productive programme' (1939: 75).

While Salazar was prepared to congratulate the dictatorship for rescuing the nation from the anarchic depths into which it had descended, he was emphatic in his belief that its intrinsic value was purely instrumental.

In his view the dictatorship could never be anything more than a vehicle for change.

He believed that it was in the nature of military dictatorships to be the creations of societal conflict: they are brought into existence on such occasions with the sole purpose of restoring authority.

Therefore, they will adopt measures that are intended to achieve ends conducive to this goal.

Once order has been restored, military regimes cease to have a function other than to restore the reins of government to responsible men who can be trusted to maintain order through the proper use of their authority.

Because military dictatorships have narrow aims, their rule must necessarily be 'essentially of a transitory nature... A dictatorship is... a government almost without supervision... and a delicate instrument that is quickly exhausted and which one can easily abuse.

For this reason, it is as well that it should not aspire to eternity' (1939: 83-4).

It is manifest that through this speech, Salazar managed to achieve two of his three goals. His use of negative terms when describing the situation that existed during the First Republic was intended to reinforce in his audience's minds unfavourable memories of that particular era.

His anxiety to denounce the parliamentary republic was primarily inspired by his belief there was a growing tendency within Portuguese society for a return to some form of parliamentarism. As was so often the case with Salazar, his fears were not without foundation.

By 1930, authority and order had been restored, and the dictatorship's work was complete. The anarchy of the First Republic seemed but a distant memory and Portugal appeared to be a different nation with renewed pride and ready to resume its place with the restored parliament.

Salazar's success at the helm of the dictatorship seemed to be responsible for the recovery of faith in the institutions of democracy, and if this feeling was to be allowed to gain strength, his plans would be in jeopardy.

It should be noted that, lacking any positive ideology of their own, the leaders of the 28 May Movement were in 1926 happy to accept comparisons with the Spanish dictator Primo de Rivera, after all, Primo had come to power in similar circumstances and intending to rid his nation of a parliamentary regime that was comparable to that which the Portuguese rebels had just overthrown.

Their readiness to consent to being compared with Primo in 1926 should come as no surprise when one considers that following the defeat of Abd el-Krim in 1925 (a victory that had eluded the civilian government for several years), Primo was regarded by large sections of Spanish society as a hero and a saviour.

In 1926, he was arguably at the height of his popularity; however, by 1930, the situation had altered dramatically.

At the time Salazar was giving his speech celebrating the dictatorship's fourth anniversary, not only had Primo been forced to resign, but he had died a bitter man in exile in Paris.

Salazar was aware of the direction events in Portugal's neighbour were taking and must have feared that a return to some form of parliamentary democracy in Madrid was almost certain.

His fear was that the Portuguese may once again wish to emulate their neighbour's example.

If his project was to have any chance of success, he had to undermine the dictatorship in a very subtle manner. He had to condemn it with praise.

As we have seen, he encouraged his audience to congratulate the military for acting when they did, for saving the nation from the politicians; but his praise is strictly limited, for he also stresses his opinion that its work is done.

While not actually stating the military should step down, he is unambiguous in his view that the military should make plans to return to barracks and hand power to the only civilian who has proved capable of dining the mantle of responsibility.

Notwithstanding the clarity of his express desires, Salazar's economic abilities and political astuteness were more than matched by his ambition for power.

Indeed, they were attributes that had seen him rise from obscurity to one of the highest and most powerful positions in society.[9] Evidence of these traits is apparent in his two early speeches mentioned above.

Not only did he successfully bring into question the ability of the dictatorship to hold onto power, but he also raised the issue of the questionable nature of the morality, let alone the legality, of their attempt to do so.

[9] It has been claimed that Salazar never harboured any political ambitions, conventional wisdom claims but he believed the nation needed him and that it was his duty as a Christian and a Portuguese to answer the call of God and his nation. The fact it suited Salazar and his government for him to be regarded as an exemplary figure should cast doubt on the validity of this claim, however, as should the fact that it is generally employed by eulogists and hagiographers (see Kay 1970; Derrick 1938; Egerton 1943). In his critical history of the New State, Figueiredo claims that rather than the reluctant politician of myth, Salazar, from an early age, displayed evidence of political ambition (1975: 19-25).

More than this, however, he expressly distinguished the dictatorship from the government. He explicitly claimed the dictatorship aimed to serve the government by ensuring the conditions for their programme.

With this claim, Salazar is clearly attempting to reclaim the praise he appears to be placing at the feet of the military regime.

While he appears to be crediting the dictatorship with the real advances made in the four years since the coup, what he is doing is thanking them for overthrowing the liberal regime and creating the necessary conditions for a return to order.

The government, not the dictatorship, is being praised here, and the power within the government was the Minister of Finance. This interpretation is reinforced when one examines the opening words of this speech:

> In our eagerness for improvements and more rapid progress, we forget all we have suffered and do not appreciate the benefits we enjoy. Let us, then, carry our memories back into the past so that we may render justice to the present; let us also keep in mind that before we began our work of reorganisation, 'disorder' was the only word that could suitably describe conditions existing in Portugal (Salazar 1939: 69).

Let us then *cast our minds back* to the period before *reorganisation.*

In an earlier speech, in fact, in his speech accepting appointment to the office of Minister of Finance, Salazar quite clearly states that only his 'rigid code… will set in order, once and for all, the economic and financial life of the nation' (Salazar 1939: 44).

As far as he was concerned, the real advances could only possibly have been made after 1928. The dictatorship cannot reasonably expect to be thanked for this; all it can expect is to be congratulated for creating the necessary conditions. The rest of the credit belongs to him, because it was he who had the programme and the fortitude to see it through.

In having thus undermined the dictatorship and reduced the credibility of any potential return to parliamentary democracy, one must contend Salazar showed extraordinary political skill.

However, one task remained to be completed. Salazar understood that it was not sufficient to cast doubt on the legitimacy of the alternatives. Having allowed himself to be hailed as a Sebastian figure through his apparent success at the helm of the nation's finances, he understood how to present a plan of his own to the people: a plan that would be capable not only of capturing the nation's imagination but one that would capture their minds and their souls. Portugal did not have long to wait.

Salazar's prescription:
The vision projected, 1930-32

After 1930, Salazar's pronouncements changed.

Before this date, his chief concern was ensuring, as far as he possibly could, that democracy became synonymous with disorder. In his later speeches, those made between 1930 and 1932, he showed a greater concern for presenting his proposals for the future organisation of Portuguese society.

His first major speech of this period was made following the announcement by the head of government, General Domingos de Oliveira, after the creation of the National Union (União Nacional).

According to a report in the *Diário de Notícias* dated 31 July 1930, the day following the meeting, General Domingos claimed the time had come to begin a return to constitutional normality and that the formation of the National Union was the first step in that path.

While the fact the Prime Minister had made a speech was reported, the speech itself was not carried. Salazar's speech, however, was reprinted verbatim, perhaps reflecting the realpolitik of the time: what Salazar had to say was important and should have the widest possible audience.

Where the Prime Minister restricted himself to generalities, indicating his own belief in the policies that his Finance Minister was pursuing, Salazar dealt with specifics. He began by mentioning the disorderly nature of the parliamentary republic, disorders he claimed were caused by the influx of alien ideologies that were 'more or less influenced by international tendencies' (1939: 90).

He claimed the socialist and liberal influences, themselves products of materialism corrupted by the ideas of the french enlightenment, were responsible for the emergence of an equally alien form of nationalism: of a reactionary, defensive and materialist nationalism.

Neither the nationalist reaction nor its cause could be acceptable to the Portuguese state, as both were essentially products of a political movement that sought to separate politics from morality.

Salazar was making a veiled reference to the Italian regime, which despite its *admirable* attributes (such as the restoration of order and the corporatist policies), was ultimately a product of liberalism.[10]

The dictatorship was praised once more but in the same conditional manner. Salazar used this praise of the dictatorship as a means of further attacking the republican regime it succeeded, mentioning its

[10] In 1934, Salazar banned Rolão Preto's Italian Fascist-inspired National Syndicalist Movement and sent its leadership into exile. Fascism, he claimed, best itself on the 'exultation of youth and the cult of force through direct action, the principle of the superiority of state political power in social life, and the propensity for arousing masses behind a single leader', and as such was a creed that was not only at variance with but also opposed to Portuguese tradition and the aims of the New State (Payne 1973: 669).

failures and the lawlessness that prevailed to stop as if to encourage his audience to believe that his interpretation was self-evidently true, he concluded his point with a simple statement of *fact* that 'we all know what we have been through' (1939: 92).

Effectively, Salazar was telling his listeners and readers to think back, but not to allow the passage of time to diminish the harsh reality that was the truth: yes, all of Portugal knew what the republican regime was like and it would be absurd to wish for its return.

To emphasise the point, he offered his audience as contrast between the anarchy of the parliamentary republic and the peace, security and order that typified his government.

No reasonable person, not even the *reprehensible* politicians, harboured any desire for a return to 'a regime of partisanship' in which all the gains that had been made would be lost to a system that, owing to its extended exclusion from power would be even more destructive and more indisciplined than before.

To emphasise his point, Salazar could use the example of the degeneration of the Spanish Republic following its return to liberal democracy after the overthrow of its monarchy and the consequent rejection of traditional forms of rule.

During the early part of 1932, the Portuguese press was keen to publish articles, usually prominently, denouncing the anarchy and lawlessness afflicting the Spanish Republic.

It would seem no effort was spared in the drive to create a bad impression of Portugal's neighbour: the press carried tales of demonstrations, strikes, battles between anarcho-syndicalists and the police, unemployment, murders and robberies from cathedrals, all under such overtly sensationalist headlines as *Banditry in Spain, Worker Robbed in Broad Daylight, Woman Killed and Robbed in her Own Home*.[11]

It was not uncommon for such articles to be accompanied by photographs of shadowy figures holding guns, further enhancing the notion of lawlessness by creating the impression that these criminals, men who could pose for press photographs, were operating without any fear of being challenged and that law and order had completely broken down.[12]

[11] One story in the *Diário de Notícias* dated 2 January 1932 under the headline 'A tenancy agreement gone wrong' tells the tale of a woman in a Spanish town who ran screaming to neighbours claiming that three men who said they wished to rent her house actually intended only to assault and rob her who stop the fact the man proved to be genuine and honest only served to emphasise Salazar's contention more forcibly. The woman was scared, and this fear, even though it was unfounded in the circumstances, was a direct result of the failure of the government of the Spanish Republic to establish the rule of law.

[12] For this section on the Portuguese Press's characterisation of this state of lawlessness in the Spanish Republic, I have relied mainly on the Lisbon daily newspaper *Diário de Notícias* from the first six months of 1932. This newspaper, which was among the most liberal of the period, may not have been as denunciatory of the Spanish Republic as some others. This alone perhaps reflects the value of these stories to Salazar's legitimation project.

Salazar presented himself as a visionary—a charismatic prophet—and this is his revelation: to wish for a return to democracy would be to wish for a return to disorder as had occurred in Spain, and only the 'thoughtless, unworthy, illogical' and irresponsible could have wanted that.

With this, he dismisses both the past and the present in favour of his future.

The Portuguese nation's unity and indivisibility were regarded as fundamental principles in this future. The interests of each person and group of people were to be subordinated to those of the nation; moreover, subordinated to a nation devoid of political parties.

Portugal's history is returned to time and again as an inspirational example to guide thoughts and actions. Much is made of Portugal's past achievements: the longevity of its independent existence, its establishment because of reconquest by the Holy Crusade against the Moors, the homogeneity and industriousness of its people, its success in obtaining and maintaining overseas territories and exporting Christianity and civilisation to distant corners of the world.

According to Salazar, these achievements were made without thought of material reward and without causing damage to the interests of any other European power, reflecting Portugal's 'traditionally pure and moral character' and the willingness of the

Portuguese to sacrifice their material comforts for higher ideals.[13]

In order to rediscover this lost morality, he suggested the Portuguese nation must reassert its independence from those *international doctrines* that have been both the cause and consequence of so many of the disorders that had afflicted it (Salazar 1939: 114).

While this reaffirmation of national autonomy must inevitably consist of renunciation of foreign ideologies, Salazar recognised this also required a corresponding foreswearing of foreign economic penetration in the belief that an important and inescapable function of the latter is the promotion of the former.

To achieve this restoration of moral and material autarchy, he believed the state's integrity had to be asserted against the inevitable attacks from those who remained wedded to the fundamentally materialistic and *amoral* ideologies of liberalism, socialism and the party system.

[13] It would appear Salazar is attempting to suggest that the age of discoveries, Portugal's *golden age*, should be regarded as an example of Portugal's moral superiority over its imperial competitors. While the Portuguese nation did grow rich on the patrimony of its colonies, this material benefit is regarded by Salazar as a byproduct, perhaps even God's reward to Portugal for gaining new converts to Christianity: it was not, however, the motive behind the voyages. Salazar seems to suggest that Portugal's moral decline can be traced to the emergence of democracy in the land and that the Portuguese temporarily lost their civilising drive, preferring instead to get involved in internecine disputes. This is the real cause of Portugal's decline, and Salazar's mission is to reinject unity and order to rediscover morality.

Salazar's state was to be the defender of the unity and indivisibility of the nation: two concepts that, for two overarching reasons, he regarded as essential prerequisites for achieving his goal of national renewal.

The first of these reasons is related to Salazar's interpretation of the nation as a moral entity symbolising the highest representation of the will of the people.

Portugal's moral and ethical unity was, for Salazar, a precept born of the nation's Catholic traditions which, although submerged for a period, nonetheless survived more or less intact: it was a tradition that extolled the virtues of cooperation, a belief in humanity, in humility, in Christianity and in respect for God's preordained natural order.

The moral nation was to be guided by the state (1939: 122), which would have the sole right to control the nation's activities in such a manner as would encourage and enhance national unity (1939: 98). Salazar claimed that this unity was essential for progress and stability, and that:

> There will be no definite progress unless it is accompanied by a revolution in the mental and moral outlook of the Portuguese people of the present day and a careful education of our future generations (1939: 108).

This *mental and moral* revolution, however, was more concerned with a return to traditional values that had been so long submerged beneath the tide of individualistic and materialistic liberalism.

Continuing to deny the nation's essential unity would encourage divisions, creating openings that would unavoidably lead to dissent, decay and return of political factions.

The second idea being conveyed by Salazar's claim for unity derives from the idea of the nation as a material entity.

The subdivision of Portugal's territory into small self-governing districts could not, in Salazar's view, be permitted, even if these districts were to enjoy minimal autonomy.

Creating such a system would only encourage dissent and discontent as competition between districts for a share of the national patrimony would inevitably follow, effectively creating new and essentially artificial differences between Portuguese.

The inevitable result of such a policy would be the return of democracy,[14] political parties and political strife led to tomorrow's degeneration and the dissolution of the nation into myriad competing factions.

The state, which was intended to be the nation's guide, would be reduced, ineluctably, to an instrument for dispensing favours and rewards to the most powerful factions, solely to sustain the government

[14] In the Aristotelian sense.

of politicians' grip on power. If the nation were to fail to assert its unity, said Salazar, it would experience both a rapid moral and material breakdown that would see the nation reduced once again to chaos and disorder.

Thus, according to his vision, unity and indivisibility were considered indispensable for moral and material reasons.[15]

To promote this unity, Salazar's project envisaged granting the state administration strong powers and removing its reliance on the legislative branch, which he disdainfully regarded to be the refuge of those who 'are under the influence of liberal individualism, of socialism, of parties and those who suffer from the excesses and disorders of the parliamentary system' (1939: 98).

The executive should enjoy the same independence of action and autonomy of deliberation that is afforded the legislature; ministers of his choosing should assist the Prime Minister and, echoing his statement on assuming the Ministry of Finance in 1928, he should be allowed to command in the knowledge that he will be obeyed.[16]

However, as we have seen, Salazar was at pains to distinguish his proposed system from that which

[15] See Salazar's speeches in the cabinet room on 30 July 1930 (1939: 89-109) and in the Coliseu de Recreios on 17 May 1931 (1939: 113-28).

[16] See his speech of 27 April 1928, when he accepted appointment to the Ministry of Finance (1939: 43-5).

existed in any other country, and most especially from the Fascist system pioneered by Mussolini, which was a system he regarded to be 'inspired by certain foreign models' (Payne 1973: 668).

According to some hagiographers of Salazar's vision, his project differed from Italian and German totalitarianism in that his was based on the recognition of the rights of the individual as a constituent part of, and as inseparable from, the nation: 'the Portuguese conception is based on a full recognition of man's spiritual nature... Which is in itself a reversion to the Christian view and a reaction against that depersonalising tendency of modern social life' (Egerton 1943: 199).[17]

While Salazar owed a debt to Mussolini, and while it is also not in question that he admired certain aspects of Il Duce's experiment, it is nonetheless beyond doubt that his project owed much to the papal encyclicals, *Rerum Novarum, Quadragesimo*

[17] It is interesting to note that in 1933, Mussolini read his corporatist programme to the Italian Assembly of the National Council of Corporations. In this speech, he claimed that if the corporatist system was 'to be carried out fully, completely, integrally, revolutionary', it would have to include three important elements: a single political party; a totalitarian state; and 'an atmosphere of strong ideal tension' (Mussolini 1936: 9-25). By contrast, Salazar claimed that the National Union was 'incompatible with the spirit of party and political faction' (Egerton 1943: 191). For him, power was limited by morality, thus helping the Portuguese avoid 'deifying the state... and challenging God' (Derrick 1938: 72), and Salazar's project was, as we have seen, promoted as a route towards the restoration of social harmony. Thus, none of Mussolini's essential conditions makes an appearance in Salazar's justifications.

Anno and *Divini Redemptoris*, of popes Leo XIII and Pius XI (Derrick 1938: 63, 104).

Salazar's pronouncements repeatedly emphasise the need for moral renewal. It is not enough for the institutions to reconstruct themselves along new patterns if the individual fails to take their task seriously.

The nation, as the highest representation of the collectivity of individuals, will ultimately fail in its renovation.

Therefore, the state's most urgent responsibility must be the revival of the moral spirit within all individuals who constitute the Portuguese nation, wherever they may be.

This funct ion was to be fulfilled by the complete reorganisation of social and economic life under total redefinition of each person's relation with each other, and this was to be achieved by the construction of a corporate state that would recognise the associations of people as the primary structure of civil society.

According to Salazar and the social Catholics with whom he has been associated, corporatism was the most natural form of political association.

It is a form of association that recognises and harmonises the individual's social and economic interests.

Salazar believed people are social animals and firmly rejected the liberal conception that this sociability is designed primarily for satisfying the material necessities of life. What is most important, he insisted, is not the comfort that comes of possessions—these are of secondary importance—rather, he insisted that an individual's primary needs are spiritual and bound up more closely in their innate desire for companionship.

While this remains a concept that contains a materialist element, it is more a materialism of the spirit than of the body.

Only once an individual's spiritual needs have been satisfied can they, with any sense of justice (or, as Salazar might say: 'truth'), proceed to provide for their physical material requirements.

The great flaw of liberalism, he believed, was its failure to understand this fundamental truth of natural law and its elevation of the physical over the spiritual.

Once materialist conceptions had gained primacy and morality had been relegated, men quickly began to feel alienated, isolated and alone –prey to demagoguery and corrupted by greed.

In Salazar's view, both the politicians and the Portuguese people, through their inability—or worse –their unwillingness to prevent the loss of social morality, were to blame for the inevitable material corruption that followed:

'We have distorted the idea of wealth…'
said Salazar. 'We have put it into a sep-

arate category, apart from the interests of the community and apart from moral concepts... We have distorted the idea of labour... and forgotten that the labourer is a member of a family... We detached the worker from the natural surroundings of his profession... Next we allowed him to ally himself with others... in opposition to the state... in opposition to his employers... even in opposition to other workers... No spirit of cooperation—nothing but hate, destructive hate' (Derrick 1939: 80-1).

The corporate state would remedy these ills by re-introducing morality into political life.

Salazar insisted his vision would not be realised overnight; however, he believed raising expectations through the promotion of false and ultimately unrealisable promises was the domain of demagogues and liberals.

The promise that his government was to be one of truth relieved it of any *duty* to give the people rhetoric if Portugal's renewal was to be complete, that is, if there were to be a total moral renovation.

According to Salazar, 'Our first task is to renew the individual himself, to transform him, to bring him into harmony with his own environment, his own country' (Egerton 1943: 169).

The emphasis on the moral renewal of the individual allowed Salazar the luxury of time—a stable system requires sound foundations—'every revolution, if it is to be lasting, cannot destroy that upon which it is based—the fundamental principles... the great realities of social life' (Derrick 1939: 93).

While he proclaimed the inevitability of the future corporate state, its slow emergence did not perturb him, for ultimately the corporations had to come from the people who could, in turn, only create them once they had been morally *reborn*: [18]

> While not one single corporatist organisation has yet been completed in its entirety, the national economy is being influenced by the corporatist spirit, which is essential for the success of the new regime. Therefore, to avoid endangering the system on the part of its administrators or unfavourable social conditions, we experimented with 'pre-corporatist organisations' before deciding upon typical ones (Salazar 1939: 21).

Typical corporations would presumably emerge with the development of the *corporate spirit* his system would engender and promote.

This assumption allowed Salazar to proclaim that Portuguese corporatism was to emerge from

[18] 'The Portuguese Republic is a corporate state by definition, but that does not mean to say that the corporate organisation is already realised' (Derrick 1939: 92).

below, unlike in Italy, where it was imposed by state fiat.[19]

Salazar's medication: The side effects

By insisting on the fundamentally social nature of his corporatism and stressing his relationship to the writings of the Church and Portuguese tradition, Salazar was attempting to do two things.

While he was determined to place some distance between his indigenous corporatism and the Fascist corporatism of Mussolini, what was even more important to him was the necessity of distinguishing his vision from that of Portuguese Integralism, a movement that was increasingly divided between moderates and radicals.[20]

Portuguese Integralism was a movement with an ideology that was, at least superficially, not dissimilar from that of Salazar and his followers.

Initially created as a discussion group for young

[19] Jacobs (1958) provides a useful critical discussion, from a pluralist perspective, of the reasons behind the slow emergence of Portuguese corporations.

[20] Payne (1973: 14-21) discusses the major differences between fascism and the 'conservative authoritarian right' of Salazar. 'In philosophy, the conservative authoritarian right, and in many instances also the radical right, based themselves upon religion more than upon any new cultural mystique... Hence the *new man* of the authoritarian right was grounded on and to some extent limited by the presets and values of traditional religion, or more specifically, the conservative interpretations thereof' (1973: 17).

exiled monarchist intellectuals in 1914, Integralismo Lusitano modelled itself on Charles Maurras's Action Française and declared itself against everything the liberal republic represented.

The Integralists expressed their support for the creation of a corporate state, called for a programme of moral renewal, demanded protection for the Church, and, like Salazar, denounced the imposition of the British political system in Portugal.[21]

Salazar nonetheless mistrusted their willingness to engage in physical, even violent acts in furtherance of their aims.

When offered an opportunity to praise the Maurrasian system, Salazar proved remarkably reluctant to do so:

> [Maurras's] slogan *politics first!* It is perfectly comprehensible and admirably sums up the dynamic of his closest disciples. However, in this expression, there

[21] Compare, for example, Salazar's statement in his introduction to the French edition of his collected speeches, *Une Révolution dans la Paix*, Paris (1936): 'One of the greatest mistakes of the 19th century was to suppose that the British parliamentary system, British democracy, was a form of government capable of adaptation to the needs of all European peoples' (Derrick 1938: 108; Egerton 1943: 193), with that of Teotónio Pereira, who said: 'we must reject British parliamentarism... our tradition is more spiritual than material... We must restore Portugal to its true nature and its legitimate power through the creation of a corporate system in accord with our own history and culture' (Wiarda 1977: 77). Pereira was later to write the National Labour Statute, which outlined the corporate structure of Salazar's New State. He went on to become Under-Secretary of State for Corporations in Salazar's government.

> is a historical and sociological fallacy that
> is by no means without its dangers so
> far as the formation of the younger gen-
> eration is concerned. Indeed, politics
> have a place... But the life of a country
> is broader and more complex; it is less
> accessible to the organs and actions of
> government than many people seem to
> imagine (Egerton 1943: 168).

As an institution representing the state's authority, the government must inevitably share the natural limitations restricting the state's lawful area of action.

For Salazar, at least publicly, the politics of government should be restricted to those functions that enhance the moral well-being of each individual as an integral part of the nation.

Overstepping these preordained constraints would, perforce, result in any government, even one that consisted solely of honest men acting with the purest of intentions, creeping into ever more spheres of action that should be reserved for private individuals.

Salazar was denouncing Maurrasianism and, through it, its Integralist adherents for promoting an ideology containing an error so fundamental that it would destroy the very system it was designed to create and maintain: an error ultimately caused by the idealism of youth:

> Salazar commented that most of these
> young people, under the spell of abstract
> ideas that seem to them of a higher order,
> are too ready to expect a miracle from
> them and their omnipotence to bother
> about their own individual education and
> their usefulness to society. In this way,
> they put the problem in the wrong way
> (Egerton 1943: 174).

By supporting a system of beliefs in which the primacy of politics is pivotal, Salazar implies that the Integralists have committed an error every bit as morally damaging as anything liberalism has ever produced.

This lack of a moral perspective on their solution allows him to suggest that if prosecuted to its natural conclusion, Integralism would lead, as surely as night follows day, to the creation of an all-pervasive totalitarian state. Salazar, therefore, wished to drive a wedge between those Integralists who declared themselves mainly in accord with the movement's principles but also felt some unease at the secular tactics it employed.

By recommending the corporatisation of the Portuguese state along traditionalist and religious lines, he was able to reach out to those moderate Integralist intellectuals who also recognised the fundamental flaw in the movement's official ideology and attract them away from their erstwhile colleagues who were, ineluctably, moving in an ever more radical direction and who were increasingly falling under the secular influence of Italian Fascism.

By the early 1930s, Salazar's tactic appeared to have achieved success with the defection of leading Integralist intellectuals, such as the young Marcelo Caetano and Teotónio Pereira, to his cause.[22]

By contrast, many of the more radical Integralists became increasingly attracted to the ideas of Georges Sorel. They were at the forefront of creating an active, secular and openly violent organisation known as the National Syndicalist Movement.

National Syndicalists openly proclaimed their support for the Italian Fascist belief that all 'life is a struggle, considering that man should conquer for himself a truly worthy position, creating first of all in himself the instrument... to build it' (Mussolini 1932).

Between 1930 and 1932, this group moved further from what Payne (1980) termed the *radical right*, believing that this ground had been compromised by the willingness of many leading Integralists to participate in the creation and organisation of the Salazarist National Union.

---

[22] Caetano edited the Integralist journal *Ordem Nova* and was later credited as the chief architect of the constitution for the New State. Pereira Was responsible for drafting the national labour statute that created the structure for the corporate state. It is generally accepted that Portuguese labour law was modelled on the Italian labour charter, perhaps betraying its author's Integralist background.

According to Rosas (1994: 176-7), National Syndicalism grew out of the Integralist-inspired National 28 May League, an organisation that was itself created as an instrument through which the radical right hoped to influence the dictatorship's policies.[23]

The National Syndicalists, led by Rolão Preto, who had been a personal friend of Salazar's, reorganised itself and defined its ideological position as one of outright opposition to the National Union.

In contrast to the essentially conservative and demobilisational National Union, the National Syndicalists were revolutionaries searching for a political third way that was neither capitalism nor socialism. Preto wanted:

> ...to radically reform the political organisation of the old liberal capitalist state, opposing it with the vision of a state that is nationalist, totalitarian, organic (hierarchical, anti-individualist, anti-bourgeois, anti-masonic, anti-communist), and syndicalist (that is, the product of the grouping together of capital and labour and corporations under the directing authority of the state) (Rosas 1994: 177).

Where Salazar claimed that it was only by basing

[23] For more on the National League, see Costa Pinto (1986).

Portugal's new political order when the twin pillars of tradition and religion that the nation would be released from the grip of individualist liberalism, Preto and the national syndicalists argued that what Salazar desired was a compliant nation, set only to do his bidding.

Believing that man must be free from any superstitions that detracted from the nation's ultimate superiority, the national syndicalists were to rail against Salazar's chosen pillars as deliberately morally restrictive.

In a speech in Lisbon in February 1935, Preto was to make his position and that of the movement he led explicitly clear: 'Nationalism can never signify 'tradition'; rather, it represents 'destruction'—smashing the old ideological handcuffs and allowing the spirit to soar, raising itself to ever greater heights' (Rosas 1994: 177).[24]

The National Syndicalists believed Salazar wished to do no more than enslave the minds of the people and keep them subjected to his domination within a capitalist order. As such, they remained implacable against him.

In 1936, the National Syndicalists were to express their opposition to both the New State and Salazar by participating, alongside anarchists and other ele-

[24] It is perhaps worth noting the similarities between Preto's words here and those of the 19th-century Russian anarchist leader Mikhail Bakunin, who claimed in his book *God and the State* that 'the urge to destroy is also a creative urge'.

ments of the extreme left, in an ill-prepared uprising in Lisbon that was put down with some bloodshed by the government's forces.

This was to prove to be the last attempt at armed opposition to the Salazar regime on mainland Portugal until the Caldas de Rainha uprising in March 1974.

With the destruction of its organisation and the imprisonment and eventual exile of its leaders, National Syndicalism effectively ceased to function as an independent political force.

The remnants of the movement either stopped playing an active role in political life or accepted the inevitable and entered the National Union and the new mainstream.

The opposition of the National Syndicalists was not Salazar's only problem. There were important figures within the dictatorship implacably opposed to Salazar's project and who wished to see the creation of a very different type of state for one reason or another.

While some of these oppositionists may have prepared to see the creation of a secular corporate state, others desired no more than a return to the semblance of democratic normality, perhaps with the exclusion of certain parties such as the communists, socialists or radical republicans.

No matter how their conceptions as to the proper form of any successor state to the dictatorship may have differed though, they were united on one point, the belief that the successful implantation of Salazar's proposals would sound the death knell for theirs, and perhaps even result in their own personal consignment to the political wilderness, if not to Cape Verde.

This both enabled and encouraged them to seek a united front against Salazar.

According to Rosas, in June 1934, there were increasingly strong rumours circulating in Lisbon's political society of a conspiracy headed by elements of the military close to the national syndicalists and liberal government officials, including the Minister of War, who was himself a serving commissioned officer.

Rosas gives a clue as to why he has reached this conclusion of a man who went on to serve as President of the Republic with Salazar as his Prime Minister until the former's death in 1951.

He suggests there had been for some time a degree of friction between Carmona and his Prime Minister, predicated on the President's feeling of marginalisation under Salazar's New State, and that this ill feeling may have been responsible for Carmona's willingness to 'turn the other way' when others may have been willing to agree to an increase in the President's powers (Rosas 1994: 173).

The willingness of Carmona to continue in office, continually reappointing Salazar to the prime minister's post, suggests, however, that his doubts were fuelled by circumstances that were not personal. In contrast to Rosas' interpretation, one could suggest that rather than seeking an increase in the President's power.

This task could have been accomplished through the simple expedient of replacing Salazar; Carmona was instead seeking to minimise the extent to which Salazar removed the military from active politics.

Salazar's statements during the period leading up to the establishment of the New State had suggested the military was to be praised for its swift action in overthrowing the liberal republic and that its work was now done and that was to return to tasks for which it was more suited.

Many within the armed forces were reluctant to accept a simple thank you before returning to barracks: they wanted to help shape the nation's reconstruction.

As a senior serving officer and one of the leaders of the 28 May coup, Carmona must have been under some pressure from his comrades in arms who were seeking to protect what, for them, had come to represent a principal corporate interest for the officer corps.

However, it is clear Carmona did not feel Portugal's reconstruction could have continued without Salazar, and consequently, he was reluctant to come out openly against him.

We must assume Carmona was largely successful

in negotiating some form of compromise between his officer corps and his Prime Minister that guaranteed the continuing loyalty of the army to the new civilian regime.

Phillipe C. Schmitter Illustrates the success of the eventual compromise between the head of state and the head of government in retaining the support of the officer corps for the New State.

His analysis shows that military officers constituted the second-largest group in the first session of the Legislative Assembly, accounting for 16.7% of the total. They secured almost 10% of the positions in the first session of the Corporatist Chamber.

He goes on to assert that 58% of these officers went on to serve more than one term of office, a rate only bettered by professors and educators (84%) and physicians and veterinary surgeons (80%).

More remarkable is that 12% of officers elected to the Legislative Assembly and Corporatist Chamber in 1934 were to remain in office for more than five terms (1979: 10-12).

In assessing their commitment to the regime, Schmitter maintains the military, or at least those who served the regime in some form of official political capacity, represented one of its most loyal supports, representing 22.9% of what he terms the *hardcore* (1979: 19).

In his analysis of the changing composition of Salazar's cabinet, Lewis (1978: 628) repeats Nolte's claim that 'at the bottom, the New State is simply a military dictatorship that was lucky enough to find itself an outstanding civilian who simultaneously strengthened and transformed it'.

However, Lewis only agrees with this assertion insofar as Salazar's state came into being out of the dictatorship. He acknowledges that within the New State, the Legislative Assembly and the Corporatist Chamber did not have much say in the governing of the state and that real power rested within the Council of Ministers: Salazar's hand-picked cabinet that was responsible to no one but him.

Lewis implies that if we are to understand the actual power distribution in Salazar's Portugal, we must investigate the composition of this cabinet.

In doing so, he discovers that five out of the nine members of Salazar's first cabinet of July 1932 were survivors of the dictatorship, and it was not until 1936 that he felt secure enough in his own position to replace this inheritance with men of his own choosing. From that day on, Lewis states, 'military men never dominated [Salazar's] cabinet' (Lewis 1978: 639).

This evidence suggests that corporate pressures on President Carmona were appeased by the continued presence of military officers in the largely symbolic legislative and corporate chambers.

At the same time, Salazar's mission could continue free from any potentially problematic praetorian interference. It would appear there was also a degree of reticence within Portugal's small and geographically particular industrial bourgeoisie towards Salazar's project.

While prepared to accept his authority, there is some evidence that, at least during the initial period, their support for him was strictly conditional.

Schmitter shows that between 1934 and 1942, industrialists only accounted for 2.1% of the regime's hardcore support (1979: 19) and that none was present at the initial session of the legislative assembly (1979: 10).

Explaining the reluctance of the industrialists to express enthusiastic support for the New State is undoubtedly problematic, particularly when one considers Salazar's promise to strengthen executive power as a means of restoring both social and economic order within a system that recognised the value of 'private enterprise as the most prolific instrument of progress and of the economy of the nation' (Cotta 1937: 13).

Salazar promised that as soon as the nation could afford it his government would embark on a programme of public works designed to improve the nation's infrastructure.

This programme was to include the construction of new roads, ports, dams and bridges, works that would benefit Portuguese industry. Similarly, he was to reject any proposals that would result in the state directly undertaking works of a commercial or industrial nature, although he was to retain the government's right to intervene in such activities but only in an advisory capacity.

The only circumstances under which the state could directly intervene in the management of a private enterprise were limited to those where the enterprises, or their activities, were financed in order to attain socially *superior benefits*.[25]

In Salazar's state, industrialists and merchants were left mainly to their own devices.

However, their activities had important restrictions, mainly concerning their social and national responsibilities.

Like all Portuguese, the industrialists were expected to act in such a manner that reflected the common good.

While their own organisations and corporations were to be voluntary, they were nonetheless forced to accept the official syndicates that were, albeit implicitly, organised by the state to represent labour within the factories.

These syndicates were granted official status and empowered to reach legally binding agreements with the employers over matters pertaining to working conditions. In the context of employer antipathy towards Salazar's regime, it can be stated that while

---

[25] Articles 5, 6 and 7 of the National Labour Statute (Egerton 1937: 13).

these official syndicates eventually revealed themselves to be little more than institutions designed to maintain the subordination of the workers to the employers, the employers must have feared the creation of the syndicates and their attainment of legal status could seriously restrict the employers' freedom to manage, despite Salazar's claims to the contrary.

It is easy to see why the employers took this cautious approach, especially when one looks at the comments made by Salazar in 1930 that he wished:

> ...the state to... undertake to unify and coordinate all the activities that make up the life of the nation: the government services, the local authorities, private and public enterprises... Side by side with this idea, there is another one, which is that the rights and the moral and material interests of the labouring classes should also be assured. To recognise labour as a cooperating factor in enterprises, and therefore to associate it morally and economically with the objects of production (Salazar 1939: 98, 105).

These remarks were qualified by Salazar's belief in the sanctity of property and profit does not constitute sufficient cause to ensure the wholehearted co-operation of industrialists. The captains of industry still felt that, beneficially or not, the state was intervening directly in a sphere of activity they believed should be left to them.

Therefore, it is reasonable to claim they feared this initially limited intervention could gradually develop into something more insidious, as the state used the instruments created to support this minimalist approach to dominate industry through the creation of holding companies (as had happened in Italy with the creation of the Institute for Industrial Reconstruction by the Fascist authorities).[26]

Constant public assertions that the Portuguese labour law was modelled on the Italian labour charter could only have raised further suspicions of the ideological proximity of the Salazarist vision and the Italian example within the business community.

Conclusion

We have examined the pronouncements made by Salazar, his supporters and his hagiographers in their attempts to create an atmosphere in which his programme would be assured of success and widespread acceptance.

Salazar's task in delegitimising the First Republic was, at least superficially, relatively simple. All he had to do was appeal to the innate 'common sense'

[26] For more on the development of the Italian economy, see Sarti (1971).

of the Portuguese people: after all, the politicians of that regime had succeeded in reducing Portugal to bankruptcy through their economic and fiscal ineptitude, not to mention their corruption.

At a time when movements that made direct appeals to both the traditional conservative and the radical right by espousing nationalistic and autarkic ideologies were becoming the governmental norm across much of Europe, this task was relatively simple, even if only because of the bandwagon effect.

His second task was much more problematic, for this entailed delegitimising a governing regime in which he was involved.

Further, the dictatorship could claim that it represented the Portuguese traditionalist and authoritarian right in the same way that Primo de Rivera, Mussolini and Hitler could claim to represent the Spanish, Italian and German right, respectively.

That Salazar did manage to succeed in pushing through his scheme is beyond doubt; however, we must claim that his programme did not emerge unscathed, and he was forced to recognise the existence of opposition to his project from elements of Portuguese society that he could not afford to alienate. This forced him into accommodation and compromise.

The fact he was forced into accepting modifications to his scheme means we can reject Salazar's claims that he was some form of Sebastian figure as mere rhetoric designed to place him above the various competitors and give his proposal added legitimacy.

By invoking the myth of Sebastian, Salazar was able to present himself as a messiah-like figure who came to rescue the Portuguese people with a heavenly ordained plan and to cut through the traditional Portuguese fatalism, or *saudadismo*, and invoke the underlying feeling of superiority that is responsible for their fatalism.

His legitimising mission was essentially designed to make the Portuguese people believe in him and, through him, themselves.

This, combined with his position as *de facto*, if not *de jure*, leader of the Portuguese government between 1928 and 1936, placed Salazar at some advantage over his ideological competitors.

Not being a military man, he could come up with some impunity and reject the notion of the continuation of the dictatorship by claiming that its successes, with the exception of the overthrow of the politicians of the First Republic, could be dated from his assumption of office in 1928.

This allowed him to accept responsibility for Portugal's renovation and to denounce—albeit in very diplomatic language—those within the military who wanted to continue with some revised form of dictatorship, just as he was able to delegitimise those whose ambition was a return to some form of democratic system, whether guided and exclusionist or not.

The fact Salazar initially failed to obtain the complete legitimisation that his pronouncements lead us to suspect he desired should not close our eyes to the fact that a regime was established over which he was to remain the unquestioned master until his incapacitation in 1968.

That his regime only managed to survive until 1974, just four years after his death and long after the West's postwar declaration of support for liberal democratic governmental forms, allows us to reach the conclusion that, in the end, Salazar achieved a personal legitimacy for his regime that is without comparison in the 20th century.

References

Costa Pinto, A. (1992), 'A formação do Integralismo Lusitano (1907-17)', *Análise Social* XCIII (72-74), pp. 1409-19.

— (ed.) (1986), *O Estado Novo: Das Origens ao Fim da Autarcia (1926-59). Colóquio Sobre o Estado Novo*, Lisbon: Fragmentos

Cotta, F. (1937), *Economic Planning in Corporative Portugal*, London: P. S. King & Son.

Derrick, M. (1938), *The Portugal of Salazar*, London: Paladin.

Egerton, F. C. C. (1943), *Salazar: Rebuilder of Portugal*, London: Hodder & Stoughton.

Figueiredo, A. de (1975), *Portugal: Fifty Years of Dictatorship*, Harmondsworth: Penguin

Fryer, P. and McGowan, P. (1961), *Oldest Ally: A Portrait of Salazar's Portugal*, London: Dennis Dobson.

Jacobs, A. (1958), 'Theory and practice of corporativism in authoritarian states with special regard to Portugal', *Cahiers Bruges* 8 (3-4), pp.11-29.

Kay, H. (1970), *Salazar and Modern Portugal*, London: Eyre & Spottiswoode.

Lewis, P. H. (1978), 'Salazar's ministerial elite', *Journal of Politics* 40, pp. 622-47.

Mussolini, B. (1936), *My Autobiography*, London: Hurst & Blackett.

— (1932), *Encyclopedia Italiana*. Vol XIV, Rome: Istituto Giovanni Treccani.

Payne, S. G. (1980), *Fascism*, Madison WI: University of Madison Press.

— (1973), *A History of Spain and Portugal*, Madison WI: University of Madison Press.

Rosas, F. (1994), *História de Portugal.* Vol VII: O
     Estado Novo (1926-74), Lisbon: Estampa.

Salazar, A. de O. (1939), Discursos 1928-
     34, Coimbra: Coimbra Editora.

Sarti, R. (1971), *Fascism and the Industrial Leadership in Italy,
     1919-40*, Berkely, CA: University of California Press.

Schmitter, P. C. (1979), 'The regime d'exception that became
     the rule: 48 years of authoritarian domination
     in Portugal', in L. S. Graham and H. M. Makler
     (eds), *Contemporary Portugal: The Revolution and its
     Antecedents*, Austin TX: University of Texas Press.

Wiarda, H. J. (1979), 'The corporatist tradition and the
     corporative system in Portugal: Structured, evolving,
     transcended, persistent', in L. S. Graham and H. M.
     Makler (eds), *Contemporary Portugal: The Revolution and
     its Antecedents*, Austin TX: University of Texas Press.

— (1977), *Corporatism and Development: The
     Portuguese Experience*, Amherst MA:
     University of Massachusetts Press.

Thank you

Thank you once again for purchasing this book! We sincerely hope you found it useful and interesting.

Now that you have finished it, we would be incredibly grateful if you could take a moment to leave an honest review on Amazon. Your feedback is essential to us and helps others make informed decisions about their reading choices.

Honest reviews, whether positive or constructive, play a crucial role in supporting our small business and enabling us to improve.

Thank you once again for your purchase and for being part of our journey. We look forward to hearing your thoughts on our book!

To leave a review, please follow these steps:
1. Go to Amazon and search for the product name or ASIN.
2. Navigate to the product page.
3. Scroll down to the reviews section.
4. Click on "Write a customer review" to leave your feedback.